Mama Bear

One winter, in the Absoraka Mountains of Northwest Wyoming, there lived a mother brown bear. Her name was Ursula.

Ursula was carrying two bear cubs in her mighty belly. She walked the snow-covered hills seeking a cave, where she could hibernate for the long winter. It was not an easy task because the snow was high that year. It covered the whole area. After walking for several hours, Ursula was finally able to find a perfect cave suitable to her needs. Puffing and

panting, she squeezed her big body through the narrow entrance and lay down inside of it.

Just as she settled into her new cave, the wind began to blow; the snow began to fall, and Ursula fell into a deep, deep sleep. Several hours had past. When the cubs were born, she barely opened her eyes long enough to see that there were two of them before falling back into a soundless sleep. The tiny cubs, Baveri and Bartan, nestled and snuggled up to their warm, furry mother, nursing now and again. They were also sleeping most of the time because they were too weak to wander around just yet.

As the days went by, the storms subsided and the cubs became a little more active. They started to move around, making low humming sounds. Ursula would wake up to nurse her cubs and make sure they stayed warm, and then she would fall back to sleep. This would allow her to conserve the energy and nutrients stored in the fat of her body, to produce milk for her babies. Besides, sleeping was her chosen pastime during the long cold winter.

One day, Orsina, another female bear who was much younger than Ursula, happened to be passing by the cave. When she heard the soft humming of the little cubs, she could not help but stop and listen. Out of curiosity, she wandered into the cave. Once inside, she saw the precious cubs lying next to their sleeping mother. Orsina did not have a

family and was always dreaming about having her own cubs. She felt a deep longing and sadness when she saw this loving picture. She yearned to feel that love.

Orsina settled down next to the sleeping family snuggling up to their soft brown fur, but they didn't awaken. At first, it was very pleasant, and she felt warm and cuddly, but after a while, she began to feel ignored and lonely. Thoughts began to swirl in her head. "What if I had a cub to play with and love?" She knew it would be a few years before

she would be ready to carry one of her own, but she had no desire to wait. She wanted a little bear all of her own now.

Rapidly, she bent down and opened her mouth. Gently and quietly she picked up one of the sleeping cubs by the fur of his neck and made a few steps toward the cave's exit. No bear stirred. Orsina felt a sense of fear and excitement. She hurriedly walked out of the cave, carrying the baby cub in her mouth.

Bartan is Missing

Time passed. One day as Ursula was rolling from side to side, she felt an empty space where she felt the presence of her child before.

Immediately, she woke up and saw one of her babies, but not the other. She frantically looked around the cave only to find dirty footprints left by another bear.

Ursula could see that the prints were smaller than her own, but certainly bigger than those of the lost cub. She instantly knew that another bear had entered the cave and stolen her newborn cub. Heartbroken and determined to find her missing child, Ursula and her daughter Baveri, began their search for Bartan, the kidnapped offspring.

They wandered through the forest, asking every animal, "Have you seen a young bear with a newborn cub?" but unfortunately, no one had seen a thing. Ursula did not despair for she knew in her heart that her child was alive. She was determined to continue the search until she got her baby back.

Weeks passed, and spring was now in full bloom. The smaller creatures of the forest were coming out of hiding. One day, as Ursula and Baveri were making their way through the woods, they happened to stop by a cluster of large white birch trees to rest. Ursula looked up and noticed a lizard sitting on one of the branches.

"Hello, Mr. Lizard" Ursula called up to him, "I am curious to know if you have recently noticed a lost cub in this part of the forest."

Mr. Lizard tilted his head to look down and replied, "No, I haven't seen any lost little bears as of late. Why do you ask?"

"Well, my son Bartan has gone missing. My daughter Baveri and I are in search of him now. We asked everyone we met, but nobody we've talked to so far has seen him. I believe another bear came into my cave and took my child away from me," said Ursula with a deep sadness in her voice.

Mr. Lizard could feel the mama bear's pain. He wanted to help her, but he wasn't sure how.

"I will keep my eyes open and let you know if I see anything." Mr. Lizard assured Ursula. "Where can I find you if I have something to report?"

"Baveri and I live in the cave near Glacier Lake at the furthest tip of the north woods. Thank you for helping us, Mr. Lizard. We hope to hear from you soon." With these words, Ursula and Baveri continued on their journey.

Mr. Lizard's Investigation

Ursula and Bavery encountered many animals along the way and always asked the same question. Sadly, nobody seemed to have had any information to share. After several hours, they returned to their cave to rest for the night.

The next day, Mr. Lizard was up very early, perched on his favorite branch of the white birch tree. He was catching the bright rays of the morning sun to warm up his body after a chilly night. Just then, he noticed Orsina walking toward the birch tree with a cub at her side.

"How odd," thought Mr. Lizard. "Orsina is far too young to have a cub of her own. Who might this little fellow be?"

Mr. Lizard sat perfectly still on the branch and observed the two bears playing together without Orsina noticing. The cub would nudge Orsina, and they would fall to the ground, rolling around as if they were best of friends. They appeared to be happy. However, something didn't seem to make sense. The cub seemed too thin, undernourished, and unkempt. He looked as if he was not receiving appropriate care. Orsina herself was young. Perhaps she wasn't aware of how to properly care for the little cub.

The two bears acted as if they were inseparable.

Mr. Lizard climbed down the birch tree to speak to her.

"Hello, Orsina. Who is your friend?"

Orsina seemed to be uncomfortable, interrupted by his question, but she obviously didn't want to bring any particular attention to herself.

She only smiled at Mr. Lizard and said, "Oh, this is my friend's child who I am watching today. I am on my way to bring him back to his home now."

"He is very cute. What is his name?" asked Lizard.

"His name?" stammered Orsina. "Sorry, I forgot to ask his name, Mr. Lizard. I don't rightly know his name."   And with that Orsina quickly led the small cub away from the birch tree and headed toward the southern part of the forest.

Mr. Lizard felt very uneasy about the situation. How could Orsina be taking care of a friend's cub and not even know his name? Something wasn't right. So, Mr. Lizard quickly scurried down the tree trunk and hurriedly made his way to Ursula's cave.

Two Bears and a Cub

When he arrived, he went inside announcing himself. "Hello, Ursula? It's me, Mr. Lizard. I've come to share something with you."

He could hear the mother bear and her cub's heavy breathing. They were sleeping soundly, and he didn't want to frighten them. He gently climbed up on to Ursula's paw, up her arm and neck, all the way to her ear. Softly he said, "Ursula, I have some news for you."

Ursula woke up immediately. Lizard slid down her body and back to her paw. She lifted him up to have a closer look, and he said, "It's me,

Mr. Lizard. I've come to tell you that earlier this morning, I saw Orsina, a bear who lives nearby my tree in the woods. She was out walking with a young cub. He had brown fur and was about the size of your daughter,

Baveri. When I asked Orsina who he was, she looked uncomfortable and said he was her friend's cub. When I asked his name, she didn't know. Something seemed strange about that."

"Oh, Mr. Lizard! You have done well. I know Orsina. Her mother and I shared a den together at Beartooth Pass awhile back. I have not seen Orsina since she was a cub. I know that her mother passed away. That was several years ago. She must be a teenager by now. Do you have any idea where she was going?" Ursula asked.

"I am not sure," said Lizard, "but she appeared to be heading south."

There was no time to waste. Ursula gently woke up Baveri and set Mr. Lizard on her back. Together they began to make their way through the forest heading south along the Yellowstone River moving toward The Beartooth Wilderness.

In Pursuit

Meanwhile, Orsina, feeling edgy and worried that her secret may have been discovered, decided to relocate quickly to another part of the forest. In a short period of time, Orsina, with little Bartan dangling from her mouth, covered a great deal of ground. By late afternoon, they were on the edge of the southern woods. Both bears were hungry and tired, but they never stopped.

The sun was beginning to set when at last, Orsina spotted Sleeping Giant Mountain in the distance. There, she found an empty cave where they could hide. That night, Orsina held on to Bartan dearly and cuddled with him until they both fell asleep.

Ursula was determined to find her son. She moved fast and purposefully. Nothing could stop a mother on a mission. Carrying both Baveri and Mr. Lizard, she bounded swiftly toward the southern woods. She had to find her precious Bartan!

The next day, Orsina felt restless hiding in her tiny cave. She grabbed Bartan and came out to play and explore the area. After all, she came here to get a fresh start, and she was anxious to make new friends. She felt this was just the place to do that. Here in this region, there lived many animals that were not indigenous to the land. One such creature was Lady Emu.

As Orsina and the cub passed by a patch of green conifer trees, she noticed Lady Emu standing high on a tree trunk. Her face was lifted toward the sky looking regal and majestic as if perched upon a throne. Orsina gently placed Bartan on the ground and picked up her head to see what Lady Emu was observing.

Lady Emu was a tall bird with strong legs and a sharp beak. Her long black feathers made her look like a queen dressed to speak before a large audience of admirers. Lady Emu came from Australia where her kind was considered to be the most powerful birds on earth. In her native land, the people believed that the sun was hatched from the egg of an emu and thrown in the sky.

Lady Emu now, settled into her new home in the southern woods. Here, she was respected for her ability to solve problems justly. She had a big heart and was always compassionate toward others. She never used her strength against others or forced anyone into something they did not agree with. So Lady Emu earned the admiration of many of the animals who looked upon her as their Queen. They often consulted her in times of quarrel or misunderstanding.

Lady Emu noticed Orsina staring at her. She lowered her head and

gazed into Orsina's eyes. She saw confusion, fear, and sadness in the bear's eyes and felt a deep compassion.

"I am Lady Emu. What is your name and why are you so sad?" asked the tall bird.

Orsina was eager to talk to someone about her trouble. Lady Emu seemed to have what Orsina was missing - strength.

Orsina's Story

"Dear Lady Emu," Orsina quietly began, "I lost my family when I was very young, and I have been on my own since then. I always wanted to have someone I could play with and cuddle. I see all of the other bears enjoying their families, and that is what I want too. Yet, I am always alone. A few days ago I went to visit my mom's friend Ursula and saw her two newborn cubs. They looked like little teddy bears, and I wanted to play with them so much!

I took one of them out of the cave while Ursula was asleep. I thought she would surely come after me, but apparently, she slept right through it. I was very scared. And to tell you the truth, I wasn't sure why I did it or even if I was going to bring him back. All I knew was that little cub made me so very joyful, I wanted to keep him. I know I won't be able to have children for a while because I am still too young. I felt that I am ready to raise a cub when I saw that Ursula had two little bears to raise. Since they needed a lot of attention, I thought Ursula wouldn't mind if I took one of her cubs for myself and raised him for her. I did not mean to harm anyone."

Lady Emu felt tremendous sympathy toward Orsina, yet she understood that Orsina did not think of the consequences of making such a foolish decision. Lady Emu understood that Orsina was still an immature teenager.

"Dearest Orsina," Lady Emu gently began, "What you have done is unjust, and Ursula must be beside herself with worry, looking for her lost child. Would you want your child to be taken from you?

We need to find Ursula and settle this issue before Ursula finds you. I am afraid she will be furious when she discovers you betrayed her friendship and

took away her most precious possession."

Orsina's eyes were filled with tears, but she knew Lady Emu had spoken the truth. At that moment, Lady Emu felt sorry for both Ursula and Orsina.

In the meantime, Ursula, Baveri, and Mr. Lizard finally reached the southern woods. Soon they noticed an old black bear near a rock and asked if the bear saw the missing cub.

The old black bear had not seen Bartan, but he suggested they speak to Lady Emu. "If anyone knows what is happening around here," he said, "it would be Lady Emu.

You can find her under the fir trees where she usually enjoys the morning sunshine."

Ursula had heard Lady Emu's name spoken before and was excited to think they were near enough to talk to her. They thanked the black bear and continued on. Soon, they approached a cluster of fir trees and saw Lady Emu with her head held high. Although Emu's face was lifted upward toward the sun, she felt the presence of the mother bear and her cub, but she needed the time to think how to settle the bear's dispute. After all, she was a bird and did not know much about the ways of animals.

Ursula turned to Mr. Lizard and said, "Please stay here with Baveri. I want to talk to Lady Emu alone."

Ursula's Story

Carefully, not to scare her, Ursula drew nearer to the bird and began to share her story.

"Dear Lady Emu. I have heard that you know everything that transpires in this forest, and you are always fair. I need your help. My son Bartan was taken from me. I miss him more than words can say. Every time I look into the eyes of my daughter Baveri, I see her brother. It breaks my heart to think she will never have the opportunity to grow up with him."

Lady Emu listened attentively to Ursula. She recognized that there were always two sides to every story. She wondered if Ursula was sleeping too much and failed to protect her cub from being stolen. Curiously she asked, "Do you know why and how you lost your son?"

"I was in my cave, sleeping, exhausted after giving birth. My little ones were nursing, and I could feel their soft, calm breathing. I was exhausted and fell into a very deep sleep. My cave was safe, and I had plenty of fat to make a lot of milk for my newborns. We, bears, are great snoozers, as you may have heard. Hibernation helps us to survive long cold winters in the northern woods. Rarely do we go against our instinct and come out of our caves in the middle of the winter.

While I was sleeping, Orsina came into my cave and took my son away." Ursula explained her story with the utmost calm despite her weariness.

Now Lady Emu began to see the big picture. She was, however, concerned with what would become of Orsina if she told Ursula the truth right away.

"And if you say is true, what would you do to Orsina if she brings your little son back to you?"

asked Lady Emu.

"I do not want to punish Orsina for taking him. I understand that Orsina did not intend to hurt me.   She was confused and lonely. Her motherly instincts took over. I know that she merely wanted to have someone to love. Please, Lady Emu, if you know anything at all, I beg you to help me get Bartan back."

Lady Emu was wise and compassionate.   She understood the bond between Orsina and the cub as well as the bond between a mother and her son. She wanted to help both of them. Lady Emu had no more doubts.   Her mind was clear and she knew what she had to do.

"Very well," said Lady Emu. "Come with me. I will take you to their cave."

Bear With Me

Then Lady Emu led Ursula, Baveri, and Mr. Lizard through the Beartooth Wilderness along the Yellowstone River up to Sleeping Giant Mountain. There they spotted the cave where Orsina was hiding Bartan. Ursula went into the cave alone while the others stood back and waited.

As soon as Orsina saw Ursula, she began to growl fiercely, protecting the skinny little cub who lay exhausted by her side. Ursula quietly spoke to her, "Orsina, I have not come here to harm you. I know you love my son, and I know you meant well. But you are not equipped to raise a child despite your best efforts. You are a child yourself. You have been without a mother for a long time, and I can understand that you must

feel lonely. Please return to my den with me and we can all live peacefully together. You would make an excellent sister to both Baveri and Bartan."

Just at that moment, Baveri broke away from Mr. Lizard and Lady Emu and went bounding into the cave. She raced over to her brother. Bartan immediately jumped up to cuddle and play with his sister, licking her, and nuzzling with her like they had done when they were newborns.

Orsina felt their love, and her heart softened. A tear trickled down her cheek as she thought of how much pain she had caused Ursula's family.

"Forgive me, Ursula. I did not mean to cause any problems. I was wrong in taking Bartan away from you and his sister. I was not even sure what to feed him. I have been worried about him becoming too thin. I am happy to see you. You can take care of him much better than I. I am sorry for what I've done," said Orsina tearfully.

At that moment, Bartan rolled down to where Orsina was standing and began to cuddle up next to her with a low moaning sound. Baveri joined him, rubbing up against Orsina's soft brown fur. After a while, Orsina spoke again. "Please take him home where he belongs. He needs your milk. I love him so much, and I want him to grow up strong and healthy. Although it was short, I had a fantastic time living with Bartan. He was the family I had always dreamed of. Now, you must take him with you for he needs his real mother."

Ursula saw the bond and playfulness in these three and said, "We won't go unless you, Orsina, come with us."

Orsina looked surprised, and stammered, "You truly want me to live with you after what I've done?" she softly asked. Ursula nodded.

"Then I would love to help you bring him home. " Orsina replied gratefully with tears welling in her eyes.

Ursula smiled and said, "I know that we will make one big, happy family."

And so, Orsina, Bartan, Baveri, and Ursula thanked Lady Emu as well as Mr. Lizard, then said their goodbyes and made their way out of Sleeping Giant Mountain, up the Yellowstone River, through the Beartooth Wilderness and back to Glacier Lake in the northern woods. There, they settled down in their familiar cave and continued to live as one big happy family.

Each spring, however, the four bears would pick up Mr. Lizard and make the trip south to visit wise Lady Emu. They would sit under the fir trees, gaze up at the morning sun and share their stories.

LEARN AND GROW WITH SACRED EARTH GUIDING TOTEMS

This book is one of our 64 Whimsical Tales from the Wild Heart. Each story in this series is about an adventure in nature. Together they unfold magical journeys, struggles, and relationships within the 64 animal trios.

Our work is inspired by working with Dream Arc Totem Codex created by Richard Rudd (Gene Keys, UK).

Insects and underwater creatures represent our fears. Mammals symbolize longings, struggles, and accomplishments that they experience along the way. Birds signify a higher perspective of the journey and present a vision of the human potential. Together they form a global archetypal matrix of the most used and highly regarded totems of the planet.

Working with these 192 animal archetypes from different guidance systems will help you and your children see true magic in nature and establish a closer connection with wildlife and each other.

ABOUT THE AUTHORS

Paddy Lynn is a professional storyteller, actress, author, and teacher with over thirty-five years of experience working with children. She combines her love for theatre and literature with her unique Storyacting programs, presenting over a hundred and fifty programs a year.

To learn about her educational programs for children and adults, or to book an event with her, visit http://paddylynn.com

Svetlana Pritzker is the founder of New Human Energetics, a system that helps you overcome challenges and live on purpose. With over twenty five years of experience in education, she is highly passionate about helping parents and teachers raise inspired, creative, and empowered children.

Svetlana is an author of several books about co-creating relationships of love and trust and co-parenting motivated and capable children. To learn about her work or to book a personal session or an event, visit www.energy4action.com and www.youtube.com/Lanapritzker

ILLUSTRATIONS AND ACKNOWLEDGEMENTS

Svetlana and Yury Pritzker have been joyfully playing with colors and textures of photos, taken during their travels around the world, in order to share the enchantment and inspiration that they find in nature.

Special Thanks

To Jon L. Lynn for his insight and thorough editing of totem stories

To the contributors of websites (below) for permission to use their royalty free photos as a base for crafting some of the illustrations for this book:

https://pixabay.com

http://www.sciencekids.co.nz